Coming Into the Light

BY

KATHLINE BRAY

Watersprings
PUBLISHING

Coming Into the Light
published by Watersprings Publishing, a division of
Watersprings Media House, LLC.
P.O. Box 1284
Olive Branch, MS 38654
www.waterspringsmedia.com
Contact publisher for bulk orders and permission requests.

Copyright © 2021 Kathline Bray

All rights reserved. No part of this publication may be reproduced, distributed, or transmitted in any form or by any means, including photocopying, recording, or other electronic or mechanical methods, without the prior written permission of the publisher, except in the case of brief quotations embodied in critical reviews and certain other noncommercial uses permitted by copyright law.

Scripture quotations credited to NIV are from the Holy Bible, New International Version. Copyright © 1973, 1978, 1984, 2011 by Biblica, Inc. Used by permission. All rights reserved worldwide.

Scripture quotations marked "ESV" are taken from The Holy Bible, English Standard Version. Copyright © 2000; 2001 by Crossway Bibles, a division of Good News Publishers. Used by permission. All rights reserved.

Printed in the United States of America.

ISBN-13: 978-1-948877-86-2

To my husband Bob who has been by my side through our 38 years of marriage.

To Pastor Jeremiah and Pastor Esther for praying for me when I couldn't.

To Lee, Kim Muir, and Ruth Bray for being obedient to God's voice.

TABLE OF CONTENTS

CHAPTER 1	Life As I Know It	7
CHAPTER 2	The Runaway	10
CHAPTER 3	The Trip	15
CHAPTER 4	The Fifth Wheel	20
CHAPTER 5	Double Up	22
CHAPTER 6	The Raid	25
CHAPTER 7	The Dream	28
CHAPTER 8	The Struggle is Real	31
CHAPTER 9	Thanks For Giving Or So...	33
CHAPTER 10	Taking A Life	36
CHAPTER 11	Trouble, Trouble, Trouble	39
CHAPTER 12	The Trip #2	43
CHAPTER 13	New Beginning	46
CHAPTER 14	Steps to Success	49
CHAPTER 15	Finding Salvation	53
CHAPTER 16	Endurance	55
CHAPTER 17	Redemption	58

JEREMIAH 1:5 NKJV

❝Before I formed you in the womb,
I knew you.
Before you were born
I sanctified you;❞

CHAPTER 1

Life As I Know It

My name is Kathline Golden Bray. I was born into an abusive family with three brothers and two sisters in San Leandro, California as a Catholic. This is the story of my life and how God stayed by my side even though I did not want Him and pushed Him away at every chance that I got but He was faithful and never gave up on me.

I do not remember much before my grandpop died when I was a little over four. My mom, Rosemarie, told me that when I was three, I was hospitalized with meningitis and they told her I was supposed to die. This was the first time God saved me. I was around five years old when we moved to Pleasanton, CA. I remember being very close to my "Pop" who was my grandfather. He died just before we moved because he wanted to die in his own house. I remember going to his funeral and when I looked in the casket, I swore I saw my pop wink at me. I started crying hysterically and so did everyone else at the funeral.

In the summer of 1967, I began being sexually molested by one of my older brothers, Kevin. My brother was thirteen years old, and I used to get scared at night and climb into the bed with my big brothers for protection. One summer night I'm not sure what had changed in the dynamic of our relationship. It started as basic touching, eventually, when I was around six it turned to penetration. He warned me that he would kill me and my sisters if I told anyone. The abuse continued into my teenage years. When I was five my parents had a baby girl, who they named Eileen. As we got older, I took the abuse for Eileene so that Kevin would not victimize my sister. In my young mind, I felt the need to protect her the best way that I could.

Between the ages of eleven and thirteen, I started acting out and getting into trouble at school and home. The school reached out to my parents to send me to a therapist, but it was taboo to go to therapy in those years. All I know was that I was angry and afraid because I was unsure of why these things were happening to me. I knew that the Lord was calling to me at a young age, but I continued to get in trouble. I had my first run-in with the law when I was twelve years old.

I cut school, broke into my neighbor's house, and spent the day inside their house. I stole a watch from the first house but didn't get caught. Pushing my luck, I broke into another house, but luck ran out. I did get caught! Another day I skipped school, bought an ounce of weed, and spent the day in the park where the police approached me. I threw the weed over a fence, but I already had joints in my pocket, so I tried to eat them. The police officer tried to pry the weed out of my mouth. I proceeded to spit on the officer and was arrested.

At the age of thirteen, I was expelled from school for punching the principal, so I came home, grabbed the keys to my parents' motor home, and decided to take it for a spin. I backed out of the driveway and had a change of heart. When I went to press the brakes to put it back in the driveway, I accidentally hit the gas and ran the motor home through the garage door. All I could envision was my father beating me to death. He beat me up all the time, so it was not a far-fetched fear in my thirteen-year-old brain. This was socially acceptable in the '70s so I knew that I could not be saved. I continued out of the driveway running into the Mayor's car who lived across the street. I also destroyed the neighbor's lawn. By the grace of God, I did not hit any people and ended up crashing into an oak tree before I could cause any more destruction. I tried to back up, but I was stuck in the tree that I hit. The police came and pulled me out of the car at which point I tried to attack the police officers and I was arrested. Charged with joyriding as well as eight counts of destruction of property, I was sent to juvenile detention to await trial. Luckily for me, the presiding judge was a member of my family's church, so I received a reduced sentence. While I was in juvenile detention, an older lady, Mrs. DeMichelle, took to me and tried to guide me. We were able to get day passes and she would take me out to lunch and discuss God with me. She eventually ended up giving me my first Bible.

CHAPTER 2

The Runaway

Even with Mrs. Dee Michelle's presence in my life, while in juvenile detention I still acted out, going as far as trying to start riots and run away. I was constantly being placed in solitary confinement. Because of all the trouble, I was put in a foster home with five other children. We used to smoke pot with our foster parents, and I ended up right back in juvenile detention near Fort Bragg. There was a counselor who had a striking resemblance to Chuck Norris and we called him Chuck. I remember being in the pool and bothering some of the other kids when I was about fourteen. The counselor pushed my head under the water as a joke, but my angry self-thought was that he was trying to drown me. I thought that I was going to die. This event prompted me to run away to San Francisco with two Philippine girls. We were in a dorm setting while we waited for the night to come. The girls and I started running as they were chasing us with dogs. I saw a good-sized creek up ahead and I told the girls to get in the water. We laid perfectly still in the creek for over two hours until they gave up the search. We then ran to the highway where we flagged down a driver of an eighteen-wheeler who let us get in his truck. We hitchhiked from Fort Bragg to San Francisco, which usually took about eight hours. We ended up on Polk Street in San Francisco where the two girls said that they knew people inside of a boarding house. The girls introduced me to Blu who was a pimp. They whispered something to him and the next thing I knew they were nowhere to be found.

Come to find out they sold me to Blu who threatened me with a gun that looked like a .44. Blu made me walk the "hoe stroll" on Polk St. in San Francisco and University Ave in Berkeley. This only lasted a week and a half luckily. The police saw me on the stroll, and I was arrested and sent right back to juvenile detention. I ended up testifying against Blu in court, he was convicted and sent to jail. I was then sent to an institution in Las Vistas where I stayed for almost two years. There was another juvenile facility up on a hill surrounded by barb wire fences. It was set up like a prison. We went on a day trip there and I ran away with a man to an empty house, where we slept together. I ended up falling asleep from exhaustion, and when I woke up, the police were there to arrest me. The man had called the police to come to get me after he was done with me.

I was able to visit home on a weekend pass. My dad

let it be known every chance that he got, that he hated me. I reminded him of my mother who was a good woman but had a lot of "baggage." I broke curfew and my dad started beating on me and calling me names. I ended up calling my probation officer as my father continued to advance on me to psychically abuse me and my probation officer called the police. There was a big bay window overlooking the yard that he told me he was going to throw me out of. I spotted a butcher knife on the counter and told him that I was not going to take any more abuse.

The cops came and took me back to juvenile detention. I stayed in this facility for another six months.

Then the courts sent me to a group home in Santa Barbara. I still could not stay out of trouble. I ended up running away and hitchhiking back to Oakland where my sister Virginia lived. This was around the time the "Hillside Strangler" was killing women up and down the coast. I thought he was safe to ride with until he pulled off to the side of the road and tried to rape me. Then it dawned on me that it might be the "hillside strangler" who was killing prostitutes and hitchhikers in the mid-1970s. I fought him off the best I could and then ran until I was safe. The hands of God were covering me because I was able to make it to my sister's house in one piece. Psalms 91:3-4 (NIV) states, "Surely he will save you from the fowler's snare and from the deadly pestilence. He will cover you with His feathers and under His wings, you will find refuge. His faithfulness will be your shield and rampart". I stayed with my sister for a while, and when I was sixteen her boyfriend sexually assaulted me. Virginia blamed me and made me leave her house. She was the one that told him about all the abuse I was subjected to in my short life, so I felt that he took advantage of the fact that I had been raped before. I was a tormented little girl who went back and forth in the system, with no direction in life.

After she threw me out of her house, I went back to my parents' house where my dad just acted as if I did not exist. I believe that he had gotten into trouble because of the incident with the butcher knife. Meanwhile, I was on a mission of self-destruction by staying drunk. I was able to get into clubs and bars because when I dressed up I could pass for someone who was 21. I never got carded when I went out. Due to the sexual abuse that I endured at a young age, I felt it was alright to let men take advantage of me. It was at one of the lowest points in my life, I tried to kill myself by swallowing a five hundred count of aspirin, but God had another plan for me. I told my mother what I did when I realized that I was throwing up blood, I wasn't dying, even though I sure felt like it. My mom then rushed me to the emergency room where they pumped my stomach, then sent me home. I was forced to go to therapy where I was diagnosed with bipolar depression. They prescribed me pills, which I took for a week, then threw the rest away.

I met a couple named Patrice and Tommy who lived down the street from my parents' house and they talked me into working for them sexually. They started finding customers for me to prostitute with. I viewed this as okay because I was sleeping with men for free, so I might as well get paid! Tommy, the husband, had his way with me. The wife was getting suspicious, so she beat me within inches of my life. I was able to escape and then I hitchhiked to Sacramento, where I started babysitting for this Chinese lady. This lasted a week when her sugar daddy hooked me up with a biker buddy of his, who got me off the streets, and then I started prostituting out of houses of ill repute. I stayed there for about two months. I eventually ran away from the biker and found a truck driver going to Pensacola, FL where my Aunt Eileene lived.

CHAPTER 3

The Trip

I had enough of being used and abused by people, so when I got to my Aunt Eileene's, who owned a motel, I collapsed at her door. I was deathly sick, so she took me to the hospital where the doctor told me that I had a severe infection in my Fallopian tube. The doctor told me that I would never be able to have children unless I had extensive surgery to fix the damage. I refused the surgery but stayed with my aunt for a few months. With the bad news that I received, I started partying at the biker bar near her house. One of the bikers and his girlfriends asked me if I could find LSD so I went to the connections that I met around my aunt's motel and bought it for them. I ended up leaving my Aunt Eileene's house because I could not follow the rules.

Afterward, I began stripping, and during this time my leg quit working, so I had to drag it. This was the Lord reminding me this lifestyle was not for me. When I was ten, I fell on a sprinkler, and cut my knee to the kneecap. I had one hundred seventy stitches inside and out and had to wear a cast for three months. The doctors said I would not be able to walk again but the Lord had another plan. While stripping, I met a woman named Mercedes, I thought we had become friends but she had made a deal with the district attorney's office to give me up in exchange for her freedom. Mercedes convinced me to accompany her to court for support.

Meanwhile, she had made arrangements for me to be picked up by the cops at her court date. I was ambushed there and was arrested for sales of a controlled substance. I started a commotion, and it took eight cops to restrain me. Mercedes made it look like it was not her that had set me up. My bail was ten thousand dollars, but she arranged for a bail bondsman to bail me out with no money down. I was supposed to make payments, but I never did. They finally caught me after three months and I was rearrested and spent a year in Escambia County jail awaiting trial. I had no one to bail me out, I thought I was alone.

While in jail, I fell in love with one of the correctional officers named Rick, but we did not have a sexual relationship. I was sentenced to time served, and three years of felony probation. While I was in jail my aunt Eileene wouldn't come to visit me, so my friend Tonya who was also incarcerated with me, arranged for her cousin Steve to visit me while I was in jail. When I got out of jail, I had nowhere to go so he arranged to have me move in with him and his parents in Gulf Breeze. His parents were Christians, so they said that we had to be married before we slept together. My future in-laws arranged for us to get married, but I had to get baptized in the church before the pastor would marry us. We only knew each other a month before we were married. His parents built us a one-bedroom apartment in their basement as a wedding gift. After getting married and moving in with him I found out that Steve had severe mental problems because he was not able to deal with being adopted. He tried to set me up to go to jail by sending a package with talcum powder telling the police I was receiving cocaine thru the mail to our home address, and when that didn't work, he tried to set the apartment on fire with me inside. He lit a cigarette and threw it in the trash can in the kitchen and left me there alone while reading. I had to jump out of the window to avoid burning alive. He tried to kill me, so I took off, got drunk, and stayed that way for weeks. I then ended up back with my husband Steve as I had nowhere else to go. He talked me into renting a musical keyboard, and while I was sleeping, he took it and sold it. I was arrested for selling rental property.

During this time, you could get out of jail if you were committed or went to rehab. So the judge, seeing what my husband did to me, agreed to let me go to an inpatient rehab facility instead of violating my probation and going back to jail. I knew the Lord had a hedge of protection around me because when I entered the facility, I realized that one of the counselors was an old drug buddy of mine. My husband was threatening to kill himself if I did not come back to him and he ended up being placed in a psych facility. This all happened in six months' time and I refused to go back with him because of his issues and the fact that I was in a new relationship. His parents paid for our divorce.

I started sleeping with a client in the rehab I was attending. I caused problems, got the counselor fired, and got myself kicked out of the program. The man that I was sleeping with in rehab was Robert, his nickname was Peewee. He decided to quit the program so that he could take care of me. Peewee was much older and worked in a grocery store. I ended up getting a job at a seafood restaurant as a waitress where the owners thought that my boyfriend was my pimp because he was African American.

The following Christmas I got drunk and ended up in Tallahassee somehow. I knew God was watching me even though I continued to make bad decisions. When I finally made it back to the motel after being gone for four days. Peewee went crazy. He beat me and broke my jaw. I had to see an oral surgeon because my wisdom tooth had to be removed. When the dentist set my jaw, he wired it shut for eight weeks. I ended up leaving this man before he killed me. I found out later that my Aunt Eileene pulled a gun on him and threatened him not to ever touch me again. I was now homeless and living on the streets. The only good thing was that I was able to keep my job as a waitress, which was the only constant in my life. I ended up meeting an older gentleman that had a house on the beach. He let me move in with him. I paid him rent, but I was still partying every chance that I got. I also started shooting up drugs every chance I got. I finally went on a proper date with a guy who had asked me out. He wanted to party, so we went to my drug dealer's house. The dealer pulled out a shotgun and ran my date off. He then pulled me into his bedroom and raped me. He was going to shoot me but by the grace of God his wife came home and stopped him. The next thing I remembered, was that I was at my friend's trailer about to commit suicide again, but for some reason, I could not go through with it.

CHAPTER 4

The Fifth Wheel

In the summer of 1982, my mother Rose Marie left my father Patrick Sr., took my sister Eileene and drove all the way to Florida to visit me and my Aunt Eileene. I don't remember the exact time, but I knew that I had just gotten my driver's permit, so my mom let me use her car. In June of 1982, I was dating a cousin of the ex-boyfriend that got me a job at the seafood restaurant. I went to his parent's restaurant where I ended up getting drunk and driving to the gas station where my part-time boyfriend who's name, I don't remember. I met him when I was working as a waitress at Dainty Dell seafood restaurant had a part-time job. I was so drunk that I ended up hitting the gas pump. My boyfriend told me to get out of there and do not come back. Then I brought the car back to my mom who drove me back to the gas station to give her insurance information. I told the police I went home and drank but I avoided a DUI.

All damages were paid by my mom's insurance.

My sister needed to return to school so my mom convinced me to go back to California with her. We drove from Florida to California where my mom drove me to my brother Keith's house and dropped me off. Keith and his best friend, Bob, had dates that night and I ended up becoming the fifth wheel. Bob had just broken up with his wife Peggy the day before the date, so these were rebound dates. Bob decided to give me a ride back to Keith's house where he never returned to his date. We ended up spending the next few weeks together before I had to leave to go back to Florida due to my probation.

Bob had a job with the federal government and used to call me four or five times a day at my waitressing job. Romans 4:7 (KJV) says, "Blessed are they whose iniquities are forgiven, and whose sins are covered."

CHAPTER 5

Double Up

I was in Florida for about a month trying to tie up loose ends so that I could get back to California and my new love interest, Bob. I was still drinking and doing drugs, but I had slowed down quite a bit. I finally got my probation transferred to California, so I took the bus back. Bob picked me up from the bus station when I arrived. I got into his Cadillac Deville and went straight to a party that was held at a millionaire's mansion in Danville, CA. After Bob picked me up and the party I went and registered with the probation office to start my new life in California Bob was a part-time bouncer at an upscale club on the weekend where he met many affluent people, as well as many members of the Hell's Angels' biker's organization.

I tried everything to break up with Bob. He decided to take me on a proper date to end things. Bob had made this date with me to make me realize that I should be with him and not break up with him. He borrowed his buddies Porsche and made reservations at the railroad car restaurant which is a train car in Walnut Creek, California. He bought me a rabbit fur coat and we danced the night away in San Francisco, California. This changed me because our relationship was a divine appointment from above, and nothing can separate what God ordains.

After a few months of dating, I realized that I had missed my period. I was not supposed to have children, so I did not think anything of it at the time. I was in pain so I went to the doctor and found out that I was pregnant. The night I found out I was pregnant I had a dream that his ex-wife Peggy called and asked him to run away with the baby and come back to her. The next day his wife did call and ask Bob to leave me like in the dream, but unlike the dream, he told her no. He was staying with me! Later that night Bob asked for my hand in marriage. I told him no. After all, I was not going to get married because I was pregnant.

A few months had passed. Bob and I, my brother Keith, and a couple of friends decided to go to Lake Tahoe, Nevada for a weekend of gambling and fun. I was six months pregnant and completely sober for one of the first times in my life. We had forty dollars to spend for the whole weekend after we rented a cabin. We also paid for an impromptu wedding on February 19th, 1983. We went gambling at the casino the night before our wedding and only had forty dollars left for the entire weekend after we paid for the cabin and the wedding. Bob gave me twenty dollars and kept twenty for himself. We went our separate ways to gamble. I lost my twenty dollars in thirty minutes. I met back up with Bob who had already won over one thousand dollars. We took the money and went back to the cabin for the night.

February 20th, 1983, we got married in a chapel that looked like one of the many chapels that they had in Las Vegas. The atmosphere was beautiful as I walked down the aisle to the song "Truly" by Lionel Richie. With Keith and friends as our witnesses, this was the happiest day of my life! We went back to the cabin where they continued to party while I went to sleep. We left the next day to go back to reality. A month later Bob and I moved into our first apartment together.

On June 2nd, 1983 I gave birth to our first son, Robert Bray II, named after my new husband. He weighed eight lbs., ten oz, and was the best thing that I accomplished in my life. All was not well though, Bob started selling drugs and I relapsed and started to party. We were making so much money that we rented limos once a month, rented cars, and bought front row seats at numerous concerts. After partying for a while, I found out that I was pregnant with my second child. I couldn't get clean for anything. By the grace of God I gave birth to a healthy and beautiful baby girl, we named her Jacalyn Kathline. I didn't know how to spell Jacalyn, so I just sounded it out. She was eight lbs., five oz. When I brought her home from the hospital my son Bobby said, "No baby, hate baby, take the baby away" and stopped talking for about a year.

CHAPTER 6

The Raid

We continued partying and doing drugs. Bob started sleeping with other women, but I can't call it cheating because I knew about it and allowed it to happen. Shortly after I found out that I was pregnant with my third child, Eli. We took a trip to New York for Bob's family reunion. We stayed at the Drake Hotel where my son Bobby got out of the hotel room from the 16th floor and almost wandered into the streets of Manhattan. After the family reunion, we went to Connecticut to continue visiting with Bob's family but ended up leaving early because I got into an argument with my mother-in-law.

We must remember all the wealth we got from selling drugs we lost, for the word says in Proverbs 13:22 (NKJV), "A good man leaves an inheritance to his children's children, but the wealth of the sinner is stored up for the righteous."

When I was almost six months pregnant the woman that Bob was sleeping with became jealous because he would not leave his family for her. She called the police and told them that we were selling drugs. They raided our house around three or four in the morning. The police officer kicked me in my back to make me get on my stomach. Bob ended up getting arrested while I was sent to the emergency room in fear that I was going to have a miscarriage. When I got out of the hospital I went home and got my Red Fox fur coat and sold it to our dealer for eight hundred dollars, so I could bond my husband out of jail. We got evicted from our apartment after that. We were homeless for eight months. We had this broken-down car that we had to charge the battery every eight hours. We decided to go to my mother's house in Barstow, California. It took us two days to get there due to the car breaking down halfway to Barstow. When we got there my mom bought us a yellow van. We lived in the van for those eight months except when the church would give us a motel room once a month, which is why we were in Motel 6 when I gave birth to Eli.

While I was pregnant with Eli I did not have any prenatal care and we lived out of the Motel 6. I gave birth to Eliga on March 17, 1986, he was breech. The doctor put his hand up in me and turned the baby around which prompted me to throw up all over the doctor. I had no prenatal care with him as we were homeless after the raid.

My husband, after a year of going back and forth to court, got sentenced to three months' work furlough and two years' probation. I was able to get an apartment on a ranch with my brother Keith, who watched our kids while I was at work with my husband at night. While my husband was away on work furlough, I went crazy with the partying. I ended up going to Oakland with a lady named Tiny to a crack house. My drug habit was in full swing. I left for a week without telling anyone where I was going, leaving my kids with my brother. The Lord was merciful because the craziness that I was involved in should have done me in. Somehow my husband was able to find me while he was supposed to be working and convinced me to come back home. I got pregnant with my fourth child and around the same time, Bob came home from work furlough. We continued to live on the ranch until section eight was approved. The owner's son just happened to be on the task force that raided our house, so the owners put increased pressure on us to move out.

CHAPTER 7

The Dream

While living on the ranch I was able to get my friends, Chris and Dawn, an apartment on the ranch as well. On the night of September 2, I had a dream that I went into labor all by myself and I was wandering around the ranch trying to find someone, but no one was home. The next day. On September 3, I went into labor and I sent my son Bobby to Chris and Dawn's apartment as they were about to leave. If I would have been one minute later my dream would have come true. I ended up giving birth to my second daughter, Jade, who was seven lbs., thirteen oz. A couple of years before this I had applied for section eight housing so when the owners of the ranch wanted us to move out low-income housing became available so we were not homeless again.

We moved to a four-bedroom apartment in Dublin, California. Bob ended up doing a probation check that night in 1988 Something in my gut told me to go home and check on the house. Our babysitter at the time opened the door with cocaine on a mirror, which he was not supposed to be doing. Drugs were not allowed in our house since we were not doing drugs, because of my husband's probation. So, they ended up tearing up my house even though they didn't find anything. They told me that I needed to find a replacement for Jim, who was my babysitter.

I found out I was pregnant with my fifth child. My husband's boss made the joke that we were breeding for street sweepers in the future. It was funny because the woman that had our house raided in Livermore those couple of years before also had ended up living in the same low-income apartment as us. She thought we were out to get her, so she reported us to the police. We ended up getting pulled over in Livermore because Carol who had our house raided by the police thought we were going to hurt her. They asked about Carol. I had to tell them it was not my fault we got placed in low-income housing. Bob and I were trying to get our lives together and wanted no problems with her or anyone else.

I had my fifth child on October 25th, 1988.

We named him William. He was eight pounds and 5 oz. Three days after Christmas the same year my oldest two kids were playing with matches and candles and thought that it would be a good idea to put a lit candle on the real Christmas tree, which caused the house to instantly catch on fire. I was in the bathroom at the time. I ran from the bathroom and got all five of my kids out of the house and tossed them over the fence in the backyard. My youngest daughter said she was cold and ran back into the house while it was on fire. She didn't understand what the fire meant. But God is great, I was able to get her out of the house with only her facial hair burned off. We lost everything but my bedroom set in my room and a bottle of wine in the refrigerator. When I ran back in to rescue Jade a flame came out of the living room and licked my forearm. I realize that it was the devil trying to take me and my children out.

CHAPTER 8

The Struggle is Real

The Red Cross was able to put us in a motel for a week. They were also able to get donations for us to get back on our feet. There was a man that reached out and said we could rent a house in Livermore. After we moved into the house, I went to pick up some crystal meth from our dealers and I had brought my oldest son with me. When I went into the house and got the drugs, the police shouted, they had the house surrounded. I put the drugs in my bikini top and the scale in my short shorts. I went outside looking for my son who was talking to the police. I yelled at the police and told them they were not supposed to be talking to my son. I then hopped into my car with my son Bobby, and left with free drugs, and went home. On the good side, the police didn't find any drugs in the house because I took all of them.

Then I got pregnant with my sixth child while living in Livermore. There was the great quake of 1989 that rocked California. It was my job to keep my kids safe. My oldest daughter was asleep in our room and she refused to get up! I had to throw her over my shoulder and get to a secure location to stay safe during the earthquake. At the time of the earthquake, my husband was supposed to be at the Bart station, street cleaning. When the Bay Bridge collapsed it destroyed the Bart station. Bob's boss had just called him five minutes before the earthquake hit and told him to go somewhere else. That could have only been God because he should have been dead.

Eliga took William out of the crib and ended up breaking his leg. This was my first run-in with child protective services. I was exonerated because my older children were able to tell them that it was my son's fault. So, in a couple of months our landlord at the house we rented, tried to get us evicted by refusing rent because he wanted his relative to rent from him and thought by refusing rent, he could have us evicted.so that he can move his cousin into the apartment. I was very pregnant in the late spring of 1990, so even though the judge said that we could stay, we ended up leaving to keep the peace. Walter was born on July 6, 1990. We moved to the Crest motel, where I fed my Walter, and within three hours he looked like he was dying. When I brought him to the emergency room, the doctor asked why I didn't just let him die. I flipped out on the doctor and asked him why he won't find out what's wrong with him. They found out he was dehydrated so they hydrated him and sent him home. I was so scared during this whole ordeal.

CHAPTER 9

Thanks For Giving or So...

After my son Walter's health scare in the first week of March of 1991, I had a dream that I was walking through an apple orchard looking for my husband frantically. I ran into someone in a brown robe that looked like a monk. The monk took the robe off his head and was a skeleton laughing "HA, HA, HA, there's nothing you can you do." Then I was back in the hotel and there were flames of fire going under each of my children's beds with a voice saying, "There is nothing you can do; which one will it be?" When I woke up, I went out and bought enough drugs to stay up for a week, because I was so scared to go to sleep. A week later on March 15, 1991, we went to sleep and a few hours later I woke up and noticed that my son was unresponsive. I cried out to God to please don't take my son, he was eight months and ten days old when he passed away. They said that my son died of Sudden Infant Death Syndrome. I didn't even think about the reason why he died. This was what child protective services said the reason was. It was the worst pain I had ever felt in my life.

The Church and some friends of mine came together to pay for a funeral for Walter. I was able to have a beautiful service for him. During the funeral, I was an emotional wreck. My oldest daughter ended up running out of the church and wandering the streets. She was a mess, so not only did I have to deal with the pain of losing a child, I had to console my other children who did not really know what was going on. By the grace of God, one of my friends left the church and went to find my daughter who ran off. During all this time my husband was still working at the street sweeper company that was under new management. The boss, looking for a way not to pay my husband the wages that he made, told my husband he would be fired if he went to the funeral. Not only did I lose my child, but my husband also lost his job because he wasn't going to miss the funeral.

Bob started selling drugs again. He ended up getting a job with Holly Sugar. I was pregnant with my seventh child who was born September 30, 1991. We named him Edward. That year we went to my older sister's house for Thanksgiving. I had another dream that my Edward was in an urn on the fireplace. I was crying boo-hoo, which was the nickname that I had given to Edward.

After this dream, I was so frantic that the night after Thanksgiving I kept waking up to make sure that my son was breathing. Exactly eight months and ten days after Walter died, my son, Edward was gone as well. I do not believe it was a coincidence that those two numbers coincided with each other. It took the ambulance forty-five minutes to get there. We then had to find the money to transport the body back to where we lived. We were able to receive help and got him buried touching his big brother in the cemetery, that way God made sure they were not alone.

PHILIPPIANS 4:9 NIV

❝ And my God will supply all your needs according to His riches and glory in Christ Jesus. ❞

Bob found another job and was working and selling drugs while I was starting to spiral out of control. I started shooting up drugs in my veins. I overdosed on numerous occasions, but I didn't die. I was not able to take care of my family, but the Lord had a hedge of protection around me even in my darkest time.

CHAPTER 10

Taking a Life

I left a suicide note for my husband since he was not home from work yet. I tried to walk into traffic in the middle of the freeway, but there were no cars on the highway whatsoever. I left at 10 PM and came home at 6 AM.

ISAIAH 14:27
LIFE ESSENTIALS STUDY BIBLE
❝ All the forces of darkness cannot stop what God has ordained. ❞

It amazed me that there were no cars on the highway the whole time that I was wandering. Bob was going crazy, and he had called the police because of the suicide note, so when the police came back, they brought me to the mental. I was diagnosed with Bi-Polar depression, and on top of this Eliga had disabilities, so I was trying to get him diagnosed. He was so bad that every day the police had to bring him home from school or we had to pick him up. The Bible says in Matthew 11:28-30 (NIV) this is about the depression, "Come to Me, all you who are weary and burdened, and I will give you rest. Take My yoke upon you, and learn from Me, for I am gentle and humble in heart, and you will find rest for your souls. For my yoke is easy, and My burden is light. "

Bob and I bought a police car from the auction that we fixed up together. Bobby and Jackie had a field trip and had to be picked up after school. I was drunk and told my husband that I was not going to be able to drive. He said he did not care, I was so mad that I hopped into the car and started burning rubber. The problem was my youngest daughter Jade had hopped in the car and I told her to put on her seat belt. I am glad that I did because I went ninety-five miles an hour out of our complex. Less than a mile down the street, I took a left turn and wrapped the car around a telephone pole. I guess a neighbor decided to bring the kids home from their field trip. Jade and I were in the wrecked car. One thing I know, my older daughter Jackie, was beside me. Looking in the window She told me that she had seen her dad standing outside the car and he was hysterical. What could have been a death sentence for me and my daughter, wasn't we only ended up having minor seatbelt burns on our necks. That was the first drunk driving citation I received.

We were still dealing with the issues with Eli. We tried to get him committed to the mental hospital in Modesto, California. The first time we went it was only me, Bob, and Eli. Eli acted completely normal, so they sent us away. The next time, we decided to bring our youngest son Billy with us. This helped us make our case because Eli decided to go completely crazy and start beating on his brother. They made him stay for two weeks and diagnosed him with attention deficit hyperactivity disorder and Oppositional Defiance Disorder. After he spit on one of the counselors, the hospital medicated him and sent us home. The medication did help, and he was like a whole new kid. He was in fourth grade.

A couple of months later I was drinking with Jim. I mentioned this to him earlier. He had been arrested when we lived in Dublin. We pulled up to the lake when he tried to attack me, I grabbed a hammer and hit him in the head with it. He dragged me out of the car, beating me and leaving me for dead in a ditch. He went and told my landlord Tom where he left me. I guess it was a guilty conscience. Tom the landlord was able to get the police to come and rescue me, but I was messed up badly. This is another example of how the Lord kept me and my life was spared once again because of His mercy.

> 2 CORINTHIANS 12:9 NIV
>
> " But He said to me, My grace is sufficient for you, for my power is made perfect in weakness." Therefore I will boast all the more gladly about my weaknesses, so that Christ may rest on me."

CHAPTER 11

Trouble, Trouble, Trouble.

On February 6, 1996, Bob and I got into a huge fight and the cops came to the house. Child Protective Services went to my children's school and took them all. Bob and I lost.

DEUTERONOMY 28:41
LIFE ESSENTIALS STUDY BIBLE
❝You will father sons and daughters
but they will not remain yours,
because they will be taken, prisoner.❞

The government had custody of the children and they were sent to Mary Gram Hall, which was a group home for kids. They sent Bobby and Jackie home to me and said they were old enough to take care of themselves. After they were released Eli was somehow able to run away from Mary Gram Hall, hop in the back of someone's truck, and almost made it back to where we lived in Tracy, CA. The driver of the truck found him and brought him to the police station where he was sent to a group home in an undisclosed location. They would not tell me where they had him, so I had to call Channel 3 news in Oakland. About an hour later Child Protective Services called and gave me a location.

At this time, Bobby and Jackie were still with us. Jackie started going to church by herself. She used to beg me to go to church with her so I attended a bible study with her and decided I might as well give my life to the Lord. I still was not fully sure what that entailed. I decided to host a bible study.

JOHN 3:16

> Because God so loved the world that He gave His only son so I will not perish but have everlasting life.

The police decided to raid our trailer, and of course, there were no drugs in our home, but I decided to give all of my needles to the head detective. This turned out to be the wrong move because the landlord decided to evict us from the trailer because of all the past drama and pressure from the police.

Currently, I was in and out of rehab because I was trying to get my children back from CPS. Bob refused to stop selling drugs because we had no income, we were homeless staying at Motel 6 eating $1.99 Grand Slams every day. CPS was trying to put my kids up for adoption. Jade and Billy were in the same foster home, but the foster mother only wanted to adopt my daughter and they treated Billy like a second-class citizen. Eli was still in the group home because of his behavioral problems. Bob ended up reaching out to his sister in Connecticut who was a licensed foster mother. She said that God told her that she had to take all five of the kids and not just the youngest three.

In August of 1996, my mother-in-law flew in to see family in Los Angeles. Bob and I sent Bobby and Jackie on a train and bus to LA with my mother Rosemarie to meet up with my mother-in-law. Ruth It was about a twelve-hour ride altogether. When the kids made it to LA, they were put on a plane with Ruth to Connecticut.

My sister-in-law Kim, was finally able to come to California in March of 1997 to get the three youngest kids. During this time the foster mother of my daughter Jade was hysterical, asking how we could be doing this to her - that we were not fit to be parents. It was so messed up that we had my sister-in-law come and get them. I told her they were my children and the best thing for the children was for my in-laws to take them to their home.

CHAPTER 12

The Trip #2

So now all of my kids were in Connecticut with my sister-in-law. I was able to reach out to my older brother to get money for two bus tickets to get there. We sold everything we had and boarded the Grey Hound with the clothes on our backs and took the five-day journey to Connecticut. About halfway through the trip, we had to call our good friends in California to send us money by Western Union, so that we could have money to eat. When we got to Connecticut, we were reunited with all of our kids. My sister-in-law lent us money to rent a studio apartment in East Hartford, CT. Bob was able to get a job in Plainsville after his old friend arranged a job interview, he got the job the day after we got to Connecticut. I started going to church with my sister-in-law and recommitted my life to God, hoping this time I could get it right. I then went to Youth Challenge, another rehab, and stayed there for three months because I missed my family. I left because my "stinkin thinkin" got the better of me, so I went home to Bob.

The landlord that was renting us the studio had a three-bedroom available in Manchester, CT that he was willing to rent to us. I had to go through DCF and pass a drug test. I complied, so I was able to get my kids back. Jade stayed with my sister-in-law because she went to a magnet school, and she was also the most timid of the kids. We had to make sure that she was fully adjusted to the new living arrangements.

I got a job at a gas station next to the local bar, so we started to hang out at the bar. The job I had as a cashier quickly turned into an assistant manager job. During this time, I was still fighting past demons and adjusting to a new life in a new state, so I decided to take a whole bottle of anti-depressants. I remember calling out to God that I didn't want to die. Then I went and told my husband what I had done. When I told Bob, he rushed me to the hospital where I was placed in ICU for three days before I was released.

JEREMIAH 3:12
LIFE ESSENTIALS STUDY BIBLE

❝Go and proclaim these words towards the north, and say, 'Return, you backsliding Israel,' says Yahweh, I will not look in anger on you; For I am merciful; says, Yahweh. I will not keep anger forever.❞

I was doing well until I started working so many hours that I started taking my kids ADHD medicine so that I could stay up and be functional with all the drinking we were doing. We were also smoking crack, and one time we went to Hartford to buy drugs and the dealer ended up shooting out the back window of our car. I tried to take my life again by taking all my kids' pills and sat down in the middle of the street. The ambulance was called, and I was rushed to the psych ward. They were going to send me home, but I told them that I needed to stay, so they kept me. When I was released from the hospital, I decided to go back to Youth Challenge to their inpatient program. I stayed for another three months.

Just before I left for Youth Challenge, I found out that my dad had died. My oldest brother, Pat, called to tell me. The year before I had tried to call my dad to apologize for all the things that I had done as a kid and that I had found God. He said that if I'm not Catholic it doesn't count. I told him that no matter what, I forgave him and still loved him. He was not moved, but I hope he was able to repent before he died so that he could go to heaven.

When I came home, I relapsed again and started drinking and smoking crack. I got another job at a food processing place and had someone delivering me crack unbeknownst to my husband. I remember trying to go to the bar for my birthday and ended up jumping off of the second-story porch and I broke my wrist. On another occasion, I got so mad at my oldest daughter that I punched a wall and broke my hand. It escalated to a high point when I left my house drunk and went to get my Jade at her friend's house. Jade punched me in the face as I was trying to force my way into her friend's house. The cops were called, and I was arrested for public intoxication and risk of injury to a minor. They wanted me to go to prison to teach me a lesson. for six months and a year suspended sentence. The judge ended up giving me a month and a year suspended sentence.

CHAPTER 13

New Beginning

I went to Niantic, the women's prison to serve my month. But before that, I found out that my brother Kevin, who sexually assaulted me, lived in New London, CT. I called him to let him know that I forgave him for the things that he did to me when I was younger. He told me in his mind we were in a relationship, but I knew to free my mind I still had to forgive him. While I was in jail Kevin died in his sin. When I got out of jail, I got a job at Walgreens. We had to move out of our apartment in Manchester and move to Vernon. So, one day I decided to take my car and go to the bar in Manchester. I ended up getting followed by the state trooper from the bar until I was in front of our new house. I ended up fighting the police and spitting on one of the officers. This was my second DUI, and I was arrested on the spot.

On June 7, 2003, I was working the night shift at Walgreens. Jackie called me saying that she was in labor with my first grandson. A lady came into Walgreens and said, "God told me you needed me. How can I help you?" I told her my daughter went into labor and I had no way to get to her. So, she brought me to Rockville Hospital where I was just in time to witness the birth of my grandson, who she named Nasir.

A month later I went to rehab in Portland, CT so that I did not violate my probation. They found me a bed in New London, CT. I did get drunk when I came home from rehab. I was able to stay off drugs for five years, but I had a minor struggle with alcoholism until I started AA meetings and going to International Gospel Fellowship Church.

In 2004, my brother Keith came to live with us. There were ten of us in a three-bedroom apartment. I also found out that year, that my mom had liver cancer from alcoholism. She called me saying that she loved me, and she would see me on the other side. I was sad because I never treated her right, but I felt like we made peace. The day after she told me she would see me on the other side, she died. Luckily, I was able to keep my sobriety after my mother died. because I felt like we had closure.

I was going to church. I was able to go on a mission trip to New Orleans after Hurricane Katrina destroyed it in 2005. We were down there for two weeks helping rebuild houses for people. When I returned, I was sick and found out that I had endometriosis, so I ended up having a full hysterectomy because I was not planning on having any more children. Psalms 144:3 Life Essentials Study Bible says," Lord what is a man that you care for him the son of man that you think of him?" I needed to find this out for myself. I was too busy trying to be what my husband wanted me to be instead of being what God wanted me to be.

CHAPTER 14

Steps to Success

In 2007 I went to college to get my certificate to be a medical assistant. I was trying to be the child of God that God was forming me into, even though I was still struggling with alcohol. I got a job in the suboxone clinic where I was being sexually harassed by the doctor's husband who was the secretary. I started seeing the doctor as a patient because she was a psychiatrist. She prescribed me anti-anxiety medication and I overdosed on the medication. I went through about sixty pills in two days and was walking up and down the busy street where I lived, in a skirt with no shoes, talking about God. I went into the Salvation Army and bought a wooden cross necklace and started walking back home. My older daughter, who knew that something was wrong with me, told me my newborn grandson was sick in the hospital and asked that I would go with her to the emergency room. When we got to the emergency room, she told the nurses what I had done and had me admitted to the psych ward. I stayed overnight until I went to an intensive outpatient mental health program. I was admitted for threatening to cut myself. I had to stay as an in-patient for another week, then another month of outpatient rehab.

My husband made me stop working at the suboxone clinic because it was too much temptation. I was trying to get a job at another doctor's office when a warrant was issued from Florida when I lived with my aunt in 1980. The church decided to help me get to Florida so that I could rectify my warrant and try to get a job in my chosen field. I took time off from my new job to go to Florida. I had to do fifteen days in the county jail, but the judge threw the whole case out because they apparently lost all the paperwork that had to do with the warrant. I missed my plane while in the county jail and I had to stay with my aunt until my husband could make enough money to fly me back home. I came home and started a new job taking care of an elderly couple.

I was still working for the couple in Coventry, the husband had cancer. After her husband passed away, she kept me on to take care of her and to get her house in order so that she could sell it. I took care of her until my daughter, Jade, got pregnant with her son while she was in school. I stopped my job so I could help with my grandson. My alcoholism was getting out of control. I was drinking a pint of vodka a day.

January of 2013, my middle son Eli was arrested and was sent to jail for six years. So, I had to try to support him during my alcoholism and this went on for a few years. On the weekend of June 2, 2015, my oldest son, Rob, was admitted to the hospital with an infection in his heart and needed open-heart surgery to replace the valves in his heart. During his surgery, he had the Last Rites read just in case something bad happened. While he was in in-patient recovery, I took a vacation with my sister and mother-in-law to Florida. When we returned from vacation, I went to see Rob who was doing well in recovery. On July 10, 2015, I received a call saying that Rob relapsed and was in sepsis. I called my pastor to pray for his healing because his blood pressure was so low it didn't seem like they were going to get him back. The nurses said that it was God because he was still coherent. He kept asking me what was going on, but I did not want him to lose hope, so I did not tell him. I had to make the single hardest decision of my life to decide if I wanted them to resuscitate him if he were to flatline. Bob and I decided on a "do not resuscitate" order. We did not want him to suffer any longer. God was with me because all of my children except Eli got to the hospital without even a phone call and we prayed while Rob took his last breath in front of the whole family. It was 9:45 pm on July 11, 2015, when he left to go be with the Lord. I didn't leave the room for over an hour. I didn't know that then, but now I know all things are given to us on loan when we reside on this earth.

I started drinking more heavily but I did start going to church with my sister-in-law. Then Bob learned that his company was going out of business, so he was going to have to collect unemployment for six months. In 2016 Bob and I got accepted into senior citizen housing.

The weekend of Memorial Day when I woke up, I told myself that I chose to live and not die. I went to a woman's conference on the weekend of my deceased son's birthday. There was an altar call. I went up and the pastor laid hands on me and said, "You need to choose to live and not die." I knew that my son intervened because how could he possibly have said the same thing I said to myself. After that day I was completely delivered. I rededicated myself to God and threw my heart into reading the Word and getting my life right with God.

I had a mandatory requirement to do community service because I was not old enough to live in senior housing, so I threw myself into community service, started going to the gym, and maintaining a relationship with God. I truly started working on my mind, body, and soul. In 2017 and I was still an active member of the church as well as the community. I had lost over fifty pounds and worked out regularly. My son Eli got out of jail and is serving the Lord. God delivered me and it may seem like it is too late, but it is never too late to feel the glory of God and feel that He has truly forgiven me of the sins that I committed in the past.

CHAPTER 15

Finding Salvation

In 2016 after my deliverance from alcohol that Memorial weekend, I started pressing into God wholeheartedly. In the morning, when I would wake up, I would sit still to read and meditate on the word of God. I only listen to Christian music. I leave it playing all waking hours in my home.

ROMANS 12:2
LIFE ESSENTIALS STUDY BIBLE

❝Do not be conformed to this world, but be transformed by the renewal of your mind, that by testing you may discern what is the will of God, what is good and acceptable and perfect.❞

I pressed into going to all prayer and women's ministry meetings, and all Sunday services. I know that if you find the right body of Christ to go to, a Spirit-filled church, it will lift you, edify you, and build your faith. I was doing this faithfully for all of 2016 by myself. Bob and I's thirty-fifth anniversary was coming up in February 2017. My church at the time always had a valentine's dinner for all the married couples. I talked to Bob about us going for our anniversary. We had such a good time, good fellowship, and excellent food. Pastor Jeremiah told us that if Bob came to church on Sunday, he would pray for our marriage. The next day, as I was getting ready to go to church, Bob said he decided not to go with me. I said "OK", and started to walk out the door.

> **PSALMS 37:3-6**
> **LIFE ESSENTIALS STUDY BIBLE**
> 66 Trust in Yahweh, and do good. Dwell in the land, and enjoy safe pasture. Also, delight yourself in Yahweh, and he will give you the desires of your heart. Commit your way to Yahweh, Trust also in Him and He will do this: He will make your righteousness shine out like a light and your justice as the noonday sun. 99

Bob stopped me and told me that he changed his mind about going. He got dressed and went with me to the service. Pastor Jeremiah called both of us to the front of the church, laid his hands on us, and the whole congregation prayed for us. This was the beginning of a wonderful thing that the Lord was starting to do for me and my husband, and eventually my children.

CHAPTER 16

Endurance

Now, my husband Bob was going to Sunday services with me.

DEUTERONOMY 28:2 KJV

> "All these blessings shall come on thee and overtake thee if thou shalt hearken unto the voice of the Lord thy God."

I contacted my son, Eli, that was incarcerated during the years of 2013 and was released in 2019. He was released on parole and I was praying for his salvation during this time. Every two weeks for four years I took his children to visit him at the jail. He started going to church while in jail, learned how to play the keyboard so he could do worship during service. He was released in 2019 and started attending our church. He is now saved and walking with the Lord. God has blessed him with a good-paying job. He had a bumpy first year out. He was in too much of a hurry to move a girl in who had her own agenda. She lied and said that he physically abused her and had him arrested. There was a parole hold but the Lord made a way for him to get bailed out, which baffled the courts.

> **LUKE 12:2-3 NASB**
> "But, there is nothing covered up that will not be revealed, nor hidden that will not be known. Therefore whatever you have said in the darkness will be heard in the light. What you have spoken in the ear in the inner rooms will be proclaimed on the housetops."

> **EXODUS 20:6 NKJV**
> "and showing mercy to thousands of those who love me and keep my commandments."

I recommitted my life to the Lord, to give honor to my son Rob after he passed. I actually have a relationship with my Father in heaven which I stand in awe of every day He gives me breath. My daughter Jackie has a lot of health issues. She had graves' disease, an overactive thyroid. She would not go to the doctor, but she had a lump in her throat that needed to be addressed. I finally got her to go to the doctor to have the thyroid removed. She gained weight because of the surgery. She was working at Coca-Cola when the health issues started. She was on the family medical act. The company prematurely fired her, but she still has a lawsuit pending. The Lord provided for her and she was able to get hired at Amazon. She collected disability through

Amazon. She got her surgery and was out of work for three years. She started going to church with her father and me where she is now a member. She is a smart woman with a degree in political science. She also has a master's degree in business. We were praying for a job for her.

My daughter Jade and my grandson Charles who is my little prayer warrior. I would not be surprised if he grew up to be a pastor. Jade started to date a good man named James. They dated for a couple of years. I believe that James is a Christian. When he proposed, he came over to our house and asked her father for her hand in marriage. Bob agreed. They originally wanted to get married in 2020. The prices of the wedding hall and all that stuff that goes along with having a big wedding cost too much. They decided on October 20th, 2019 I was truly blessed. It was a wonderful wedding. I met up with the wedding party at the Simsbury Inn. Where the bridal party stayed the night before. The bridal party had their hair and makeup done professionally. I'm in awe of what the Lord did and is still doing in my life. As long as I am breathing, I will put my hope in Jesus that can change and renew us. I am living proof.

CHAPTER 17

Redemption

After the wedding, the Lord touched the heart of my youngest son William and his family. They started going to church. William convinced me to go to a church called Redeeming the Time, in Massachusetts. The new year came, and we spent it in church. March of 2020, the pandemic hit. The world was in chaos and confusion. It was hard trying to figure out how the church could connect and pray together.

> 1 THESSALONIANS 5:5-8 NIV
>
> **"**You are all children of light and children of the day. We don't belong to the night, nor the darkness, so then let's not sleep, as the rest do, but let's watch and be sober. For those who sleep, sleep in the night, and those who are drunk are drunk in the night. But since we belong to the day let's be sober, putting on the breastplate of faith and love and for a helmet, the hope of salvation.**"**

Our state was completely shut down. We could only go to work or the grocery store. Pastor and senior Clergy took turns hosting service to an empty church. All services were now online or on YouTube. The government, from the highest level, was not doing what needed to be done for the country. Racial tensions were in full swing at the same time. People were protesting, police were killing my black brothers and sisters. The devil thought he had one up on the church, but not so, first, remember Christ died on the cross so the devil was defeated.

> **PSALMS 33:18-19**
> "Behold Yahweh's eye is on those who fear Him, on those who hope in His loving kindness to deliver their soul from death to keep them alive in famine."

All our prayer meetings were and still are on the phone, we're able to go to Sunday service where everyone's wearing masks and socially distancing from everyone that doesn't live in the same household. What the devil meant for evil God turned it all around for His glory.

> **GENESIS 50:20 AMP**
> "You meant evil against me, but God used it for good."

I'm talking about my son Rob being taken away from me. I know now that all three of my sons Walter, Edward and Rob were gifts to me from God and no matter how long they lived it was a blessing to have the time I did have with them. I know one day I will be in paradise with them.

Why did God save me and not save other people? I am not sure.

EPHESIANS 1:7

> In Him, we have redemption through His blood, the forgiveness of sins, in accordance with the riches of God's grace.

Other Bible references to this are Galatians 1:4 and Galatians 2:20. What God has done for me He can do for anyone.

ACTS 10:34

> Peter began to speak; Now I understand that God doesn't show favoritism.

In other words, anyone that is in bondage to the things of this world and wants to be free from them can be freed by giving their life to Christ. Start following God's blueprint, which is every word in the Bible.

HEBREWS 4:12

> For the word of God is alive and active.
> Sharper than a two-edged sword,
> it penetrates even to dividing soul and spirit,
> joints and marrow; it judges the thoughts
> and attitudes of the heart.

People who are not saved have the misconception that Christians have it easy, but that's far from the truth. Christianity is a daily battle in the spirit that we have to give to the Lord daily. We fall short daily, but

LAMENTATIONS 3:22-23

❝It is because of Yahweh's loving kindnesses that we are not consumed because His compassion doesn't fail. They are new every morning. Great is your faithfulness.❞

This is why we need to retrain our minds with the word of God, and then we can live in His glorious light. It sounds easier than it is when you go through the valleys of life or hardships.

NEHEMIAH 8:10

❝Then he said to them, Go your way. Eat the fat, drink the sweet, and send portions to him for whom nothing is prepared, for today is holy to our Lord. Don't be grieved, for the joy of the Lord is our strength.❞

Infant Edward M. Bray dies

Edward Michael Bray, 2-month-old son of Robert and Kathline Bray of Tracy, died Nov. 29 at a relative's home in San Andreas after a short illness.

Born in Manteca, the Bray infant was the brother of Robert Jr., Jacalyn, Eliga, Jade and Wiliam Bray of Tracy; and the grandson of Rosemary Carbon of Barstow, Patrick Golden of Ravensdale and Eliga and Ruth Bray of Connecticut. He was peceded in death by a brother, Walter Bray, who died in March.

P.L. Fry & Son Funeral Service of Manteca is handling funeral arrangements.

Contributions are being sought by the family to defray burial expenses. They may be made to P.L. Fry & Son through the Edward M. Bray Fund.

Thursday, Dec. 5

1:08 a.m. — Emergency medical call at the 400 block of East 11th Street.

3:41 a.m. — Emergency medical call at the 100 block of East 21st Street.

5:30 a.m. — Emergency medical call at the 2000 block of Lincoln Avenue.

10:51 a.m. — Vehicle accident at 11th Street and Chrisman Road.

12:06 p.m. — Emergency medical call at the 100 block of East Grant Line Road

4:29 p.m. — Emergency medical call at 11th Street and Kasson Road.

IN MEMORY OF
ROBERT L. "ROB" BRAY II

Obituary for Robert Bray

Robert L. "Rob" Bray II, 32, of Bristol, died unexpectedly Saturday July 11, 2015 at John Dempsey Medical Center. Rob was born June 2, 1983 in Walnut Creek, CA, son of Robert L. Bray Sr. and Kathline (Golden) Bray of Vernon. He was employed with Connecticut Spring and Stamping of Farmington. Rob was a devoted father and family member who was passionate about politics and history. In addition to his parents he is survived by his fiancée, Alicia France and daughter Makaya both of Bristol, his paternal grandmother, Ruth Bray and grandfather, the late Eliga Bray. He also leaves four sisters and brothers, Jacalyn Bray of Vernon, Eliga Bray of Enfield, Jade Bray of Vernon and William Bray of East Hartford, one Aunt, Kimberly Murr and her husband Leroy of East Windsor, four uncles, Keith Golden of Vernon, Keith Bray of Holt, NY, the late Lawrence Bray and the late Ronald Bray and numerous nieces, nephews and cousins. Rob was predeceased by two brothers, Walter L. Bray and Edward M. Bray. Funeral services will be held Tuesday July 21, 2015 at 7:00 pm at the Holmes Funeral Home, 400 Main St., Manchester. Calling hours will be held Tuesday from 5:00 PM until the time of the service. Burial will be private. Memorial donations may be made to the Bray family. To sign the online register book go to www.holmes-watkinsfuneralhomes.com

Coming Into The Light | **63**

Tuesday rites for Tracy infant

Funeral services will be conducted here Tuesday afternoon for Walter Edward Bray, 8-month-old son of Robert and Kathline Bray of Tracy.

The infant, a native of Tracy, died Friday at the family home in Tracy.

He was the brother of Robert Lee Bray Jr., Eliga Bray II, William David Bray, Jacalyn Kathline Bray and Jade Bray, all of Tracy.

Tuesday's services will begin at 2 p.m. at Hotchkiss Mortuary, 5 W. Highland Ave., followed by graveside rites at Tracy Cemetery.

Visitation at the mortuary will be today from noon to 7 p.m.

C-2 **CC-TV** Friday, December 30, 1988

IN BRIEF

BART sponsoring annual safe holiday parties

Early celebrants of the New Year may enjoy free coffee, cookies and doughnuts at 11 BART stations between 7 and 11 tonight at the annual safe holiday New Year's Eve parties sponsored by the rapid transit district. The parties are co-hosted by local community groups which have volunteered to serve. BART trains will operate on a Saturday schedule until 2 a.m. tomorrow. Eastbound trains will arrive at downtown San Francisco stations at about 2:15 a.m. Westbound trains and trains on the Richmond/Fremont line will arrive in downtown Oakland stations at about 2:30 a.m. On New Year's Eve, trains will run past midnight New Year's Eve, until 2 a.m. New Year's Day. BART will run on but two lines after 6 p.m. Saturday, the Richmond-Fremont and Concord-Daly City lines.

Old building spared thanks to firefighters

Quick action yesterday by the Oakland Fire Department saved an old building at 1718-1724 Broadway when fire broke out in an artist's studio on the third floor of the four-story building. A security guard spotted smoke coming out of the window at the wood building and called the fire department, said Assistant Fire Chief Al Sigwart. The two-alarm blaze, fought by 45 firefighters using 10 pieces of equipment, caused an estimated $100,000 damage. Most of the damage was to the third floor, but some occurred on the second floor due to burning debris falling through the floor. The building housed The Holmes Book Co. during the mid-1960s. Cause of the fire is under investigation.

House sitter escapes fire in Alamo

ALAMO — A two-alarm fire reported at 9:30 a.m yesterday caused an estimated $200,000 damage to a house at 1008 Ad-

Bray with her children, from left, Jackie, 4, Jade, 1, Billy, 2 months, and Bobby, 5.

Mom rescues children from burning house

By John Miller
The Tribune

DUBLIN — Christmas celebration was cut short for the Bray family, who lost all their possessions and nearly their lives in a Wednesday night fire that destroyed their Dougherty Road apartment.

Yesterday, firefighters bearing toys dropped by the American Red Cross office in Livermore, where Cathy Bray, 26, and her five children, who range in age from 2 months to 5 years, sought shelter.

Bray, who literally threw her children out the back door as flames licked around her, said they are all lucky to be alive.

"I moved so fast, I don't remember anything except counting my children to make sure I got them all out," Bray said, still numb from the harrowing experience.

She said she doesn't know

HOW TO HELP

■ Persons wishing to help may contact the Red Cross at 443-3910 or 533-2321.

how the fire started.

A spokeswoman said the fire is under investigation, but is believed to have started when one of the children attempted to place a lighted candle on the Christmas tree.

"I went to the rest room and when I got back almost the whole front room was in flames," she recounted. "I just barely got all the kids out."

Bray said she had to toss her children over a locked gate to neighbors waiting on the other side. She ran into the flaming apartment twice to rescue her frightened youngsters.

"The neighbors helped me get them over the fence because the back gate was locked," she said. "The kids were screaming pretty loud. That's how I got the attention of neighbors."

The Dougherty Regional Fire Authority estimated the loss at $80,000, including $20,000 in personal belongings.

None of the children were injured, but Bray received a second-degree burn on her arm. No other structures were involved in the apartment complex. Most of the tenants are low-income working people.

Bray's husband, Robert, a street sweeper, was working when the fire broke out at 7:20 p.m.

The Brays will be put up at a Livermore motel until permanent housing is found for them.

www.ingramcontent.com/pod-product-compliance
Lightning Source LLC
Chambersburg PA
CBHW052123110526
44592CB00013B/1733